STRENGTHEN
YOUR

LESSONS FROM PAUL'S WALK WITH THE LORD

WALK

JASON SYKORA

XULON PRESS

Xulon Press
555 Winderley Pl, Suite 225
Maitland, FL 32751
407.339.4217
www.xulonpress.com

Paperback ISBN-13: 978-1-66289-795-5
eBook ISBN-13: 978-1-662897-962-

A Debt of Gratitude

First, I would like to thank God the Father, Jesus Christ the Son, and the Holy Spirit for inspiring me to write this book. I am grateful to my wonderful wife and daughters, who have supported me during this writing process. I thank Pastors Jeff and Tucker for mentoring me throughout this process. I also want to thank my small group members for lending their insights and willingness to allow the Holy Spirit to speak through them—a huge thanks to Geom, Gregg, Beezy, David, and Vern.

I especially want to thank Harvest Ministries and Greg Laurie. The Lord has used your ministry to speak into my life in so many ways I cannot express how grateful I am to you. Because of Harvest Ministries, the Holy Spirit helped me launch Abiding in the Faith Ministries. I thank everyone who has helped me realize my gift to help make God known. Thank you for supporting Abiding in the Faith Ministries. Without your support, this book would not have been possible.

As you read the following pages, I pray that the Lord will speak to you and strengthen your walk with Christ.

God bless you!
Jason Sykora

Contents

Introduction

Imagine going back to the beginning of time to the garden of Eden. It is a cool, crisp fall day; the temperatures are in the 70s, with a calm wind blowing through the trees. The sun is out, and there is not a single cloud in the sky. You walk alone along a trail, enjoying your time in God's creation, listening to the birds sing and the crickets chirp. Then you hear someone walking in the woods and look around to see who is with you. As Adam and Eve did in the garden long ago, you notice the Lord God walking in the garden. You desire to run up and walk alongside him, but no matter how much you try to get close, you never seem able to catch up. You realize that you need to yell out to get him to stop so that you can join him. The Lord stops when he hears the yell, turns around, and looks intently into your eyes. He says that the only way to get close to him, and be able to walk alongside him, is if you believe in his Son, Jesus. You stop and process what the Lord God just said, and you are faced with two choices. The first choice is to accept that the only way to get to God is through Jesus. The second, you can continue to run and try to catch up to God. Which way would you choose?

Hopefully, you are reading this book with a desire to strengthen your walk with Christ. But if you do not know who Jesus Christ is, or what it means to place your faith in him, begin reading the last chapter before continuing. Why? Because having a life worth living is a life that pursues a closer relationship with Jesus Christ, but first, you need to accept him as Lord and Savior. God wants to have a close relationship with his children. He wants you to grow in your Christian walk with Jesus. The pursuit of Jesus is not a sprint but is developed over time as you take one step at a time.

Followers of Christ want to be equipped to "walk in a manner worthy of the Lord," as Paul describes in Colossians 1:10. But how do we do this? Are there models we can follow to truly gain insight into how to walk in this manner? There are answers to these questions in Scripture, and from the lives of those recorded in it, we can learn to walk worthy of the Lord.

An example of a person who had a close walk with Jesus is the apostle Paul. Paul's walk with Jesus did not start well, but it ended with Jesus having a significant impact on his life. When Saul of Tarsus, a Pharisee (later known by his Roman name, Paul) first met Jesus on the road to Damascus, his encounter with the Messiah changed his life. In the book of Acts, Luke (one of Paul's companions) recorded Paul's testimony as he spoke to the tribunal in Jerusalem.

> Then Paul said, *"As I was on the road, approaching Damascus about noon, a very bright light from heaven suddenly shone down around me. I fell to the ground and heard a voice saying to me, '**Saul, Saul, why are you persecuting me?**'* "'Who are you, lord?' I asked. *"And the voice replied, '**I am Jesus the Nazarene, the one you are persecuting.**' The people with me saw the light but didn't understand the voice speaking to me.* "I asked, 'What should I do, Lord?' *"And the Lord told me, '**Get up and go into Damascus, and there you will be told everything you are to do.**'* "I was blinded by the intense light and had to be led by the hand to Damascus by my companions to a man named Ananias who lived there. He was a godly man, deeply devoted to the law, and well regarded by all the Jews of Damascus. He came and stood beside me and said, 'Brother Saul, regain your sight.' And at that very moment I could see him!*
>
> *"Then he told me, 'The God of our ancestors has chosen you to know his will and to see the Righteous One and hear him speak. For you are to be his witness, telling everyone what you have seen and heard. What are you waiting for? Get up and be baptized. Have your sins washed away by calling on the name of the Lord.'* Acts 22:6–16 NLT

Jesus chose Paul to be a witness, telling everyone what he had seen and heard. After this event, Paul's walk with God took on a whole new meaning. God opened his eyes, and Paul realized he must repent of his sins and follow Christ fully.

To repent of your sins means to make a turn. When you repent, you realize you are a sinner and abruptly stop the direction of your life and go in the opposite direction. Paul abruptly stopped on the road to Damascus when he encountered the living Savior and began to walk in a different direction. Paul's walk with Christ started with a bang, but Paul still had to learn what it meant to follow Christ daily for the rest of his life.

Paul's walk with Christ developed over time, and Paul grew close to Jesus as he obeyed his word and lived out the Christian walk. Paul's walk with Christ was not smooth sailing. Paul experienced time in prison, was beaten for his faith, was shipwrecked, faced many dangers, and endured sleepless nights. He was hungry and thirsty, and sometimes, he did not even have enough clothes to keep warm. Yet through all these unfortunate circumstances, Paul walked with Christ and had confidence in who his Lord was. If we want to learn how to walk closely with Jesus through life, there is no better example to begin with than the apostle Paul.

Paul became a witness and spoke about the Lord everywhere he went. Paul planted churches, discipled their leaders, taught the Word of God, and gave them an example of how the Christian walk with Christ should be lived. Luckily for us, Paul had written letters to the Churches, reminding them how to have a walk worthy of the Lord and his calling for us. In these New Testament letters, we learn Paul's lessons on how to walk with the Lord. As we continue through the following few chapters, we will look at these lessons and learn how to apply them to our walk with Jesus Christ.

Walk by Faith, Not by Sight

2 Corinthians 5:7 ESV
"For we walk by faith, not by sight."

If you have ever passed a section of religious sayings and crosses while shopping at a retail outlet, you have probably come across this verse, 2 Corinthians 5:7, which tells us to walk by faith, not sight. One day, I passed by a cross with this verse imprinted on it, and I thought, "What did the apostle Paul mean when he wrote it down to the Corinthian church? What meaning did it have for the Corinthian's walk with Jesus, and what purpose should it have for us today in our walk with the Lord?"

If anyone in the Bible lived out the statement that we walk by faith and not by sight, it would have been the apostle Paul. Paul became the Lord's chosen vessel on the Damascus Road to bring the gospel to the Gentiles. Once he received his orders from God to spread the gospel, he did not receive a road map or directions. Paul was given guidance from the Lord and responded in faith. Paul responded by being obedient and set out to fulfill what God called him to do. As Paul set out to spread the gospel, he walked by faith, not knowing what was ahead of him as he continued his journey. Paul lived out what it is like to walk by faith, not sight. In this chapter, we will look at Paul's life and gain insight into how we, too, can learn to walk by faith and not by sight.

Before we can learn to walk by faith and not by sight, we need to understand what faith is from a biblical standpoint and what faith is not. Faith is having complete trust or confidence in someone or something.

This kind of faith is generated from within each one, and once we confirm the reliability of what, or who, we trust, we respond in faith. We can place our faith in politicians, the government, or the voting system. We can act in good faith toward another person or lose faith in that person. Our responses in faith are exercised daily in how we place our faith. We put our faith in our vehicles every time we turn the key. We place faith in that chair when we sit down. We can put our faith in our careers and the stock market; others will place their faith in their religions.

I had a coworker who worked for her employer for many years. She was a successful store manager whom you could go to for advice and direction regarding company matters. She was one of a kind, a person who could be counted on when requested to help with needs at other stores. Then, one day, she called me to say goodbye. She had put in her notice because she had lost faith in the company and its leadership. Once faith is lost, faith is lost for good. At that point, her job was not about the biweekly paycheck, the bonuses, or the work-life balance. Her employer lost a good employee because of their unreliability. She had placed her faith in a reliable company, and once she lost faith in their reliability, she left. Her situation gives us an example of putting our faith in something generated within us. But this kind of faith is not what biblical faith is.

A good definition of biblical faith in the Bible is Hebrews 11:1 NLT, "Faith shows the reality of what we hope for; it is the evidence of things we cannot see." The Greek word used for faith in this passage is *pistis*. This word describes faith as a gift from God, not something people can produce. When we go one step further and look at the root word for *pistis*, the term *peitho* means to persuade or be persuaded. We can summarize the word for faith in Scripture this way. That is, having a biblical faith comes from God through divine persuasion.[1] When God persuades you to act, you respond in faith. This persuasion, or being prompted by the Holy Spirit, can be acted on or ignored.

God persuaded Moses through a burning bush. God persuaded Peter through a vision to bring the gospel's good news to Cornelius.

God influenced Noah to build a boat. God persuaded Abraham to leave his native land. There are numerous examples throughout Scripture whereby God's children responded in faith by the prompting of the Holy Spirit.

When the apostle Paul met the Lord on the Damascus Road, Jesus persuaded him to be his witness to Jews and Gentiles alike. After God persuaded Paul, Paul became blinded and had to be led into Damascus. Talk about walking by faith and not by sight! Once he arrived at the city, he was met by a disciple of God named Ananias. Ananias confirmed to Paul that he had met the Lord Jesus and was sent by God so Paul could regain his sight. As Ananias laid his hands on Paul and prayed for him, his eyes opened immediately, and Paul placed his faith in Jesus Christ. God divinely persuaded Paul to believe in Jesus Christ. Paul responded with biblical faith and was obedient to the call. As a Christian, you should not have to think hard to remember when the Lord has prompted you to act. In those times of prompting, lives are changed, and purpose is established.

Walking through life is difficult when you do not have a purpose. If you search the Internet, you can read many stories of people who have found their career purpose. I read an article about a professional wrestler whose children found their purpose on the football field instead of a wrestling ring. A female rapper found her purpose by using her successful career to launch foundations to help support teens and children in need. She said she "feels like her purpose is bigger than booty-shaking singles."[2] David Green, the owner of Hobby Lobby, has found his purpose in gifting 50 percent of his earnings to charitable organizations that help share the gospel of Jesus Christ.

While you can find your purpose in your career, these individuals find a purpose for their lives that is bigger than their chosen field. If you have been a believer in Jesus Christ from your youth or even a mature Christian in your walk, I'm sure you can think of a time when you had a Damascus Road experience—an experience when the Lord revealed his specific purpose for your life.

For the apostle Paul, the Lord told him to *"tell people that you have seen me and tell them what I will show you in the future. And I will rescue you from both your people and the Gentiles. Yes, I am sending you to the Gentiles to open their eyes so that they may turn from darkness to light and from the power of Satan to God. Then they will receive forgiveness for their sins and be given a place among God's people, who are set apart by faith in me"* (Acts 26:16–18 NLT).

Then what? Now that Paul has been given direction from the Lord, what should his next steps be? What about our steps? For the apostle, he began to tell others that Jesus Christ was the Messiah that the Jews had been looking for. Paul's mission in life had changed, and he was given a new purpose. His new objective was to tell others about the risen Savior.

Before Paul met God on the Damascus Road, his mission and purpose as a zealous Pharisee was to go from town to town and eradicate anyone who claimed to be a follower of "the way." Now, instead of eliminating followers of Jesus, Paul had become one. Phase two of God's plan for Paul's life had now begun. Paul went forward, fulfilling his part of God's plan for his life. Paul's purpose had changed, and he now would minister from city to city, telling others about Jesus Christ with each step he took. In each town, Paul ministered. Paul walked by faith on each road he traveled.

We are all on this earth for a purpose, and the Lord designed it that way. Proverbs 16:4 reminds us, *"The Lord has made everything for his own purposes."* God created everything around you for a purpose, and that includes you! The Bible contains many verses about purpose, and I will highlight just a few.

1. What Is God's Primary Purpose?

God's primary purpose is *"to unite all things in him, things in heaven and things on earth"* (Ephesians 1:9 ESV). To accomplish this purpose, He had to send His Son, Jesus, to this earth to fulfill this purpose.

2. God's Primary Purpose for Us Can Be Rejected

John 3:18 continues by saying, *"Whoever believes in him is not condemned, but whoever does not believe is condemned already, because he has not believed in the name of the only Son of God."* Before Jesus's ministry began, God had sent John the Baptist to prepare the way for Jesus. John's ministry was to baptize people with water, preparing them for later when the spirit would baptize them. Many people would come to John to get baptized, but some religious leaders thought differently. Luke 7:30 records that *"the Pharisees and the lawyers rejected the purpose of God for themselves, not having been baptized by him."* When God calls us into a relationship with his Son Jesus, we have a choice. We can be like the Pharisees and reject the purpose of God for ourselves, or we can accept it.

3. We Walk According to God's Purpose

A well-known passage that both Christians and unbelievers know is Romans 8:28. The verse says, *"And we know that God causes everything to work together for the good of those who love God and are called according to his purpose for them."*

"Okay, so what is God's purpose for me?" you may ask. To understand our purpose, we need to include Romans 8:29–30. *"For God knew his people in advance, and <u>he chose them to become like his Son</u> so that his Son would be the firstborn among many brothers and sisters. And having chosen them, <u>he called them to come to him</u>. And having called them, he gave them right standing with himself. And having given them right standing, he gave them his glory"* (underline mine).

If you are a Christian, one of our purposes in this life is to glorify God by living a righteous life. When we walk by faith and not sight, we walk to become molded into a life replicating Jesus Christ.

Then, finally, God's purpose in all this was to use *"the church to display his wisdom in its rich variety to all the unseen rulers and authorities* in the heavenly places" (Ephesians 3:10). We have the unique purpose of making God known by sharing the faith that we have in Jesus Christ.

Walking by Faith Requires an Eternal Focus

By the end of Paul's Damascus Road experience, Paul was divinely persuaded to place his faith in Jesus Christ. God then spoke to Paul and gave him an eternal purpose. As a new believer in Jesus Christ, Paul became excited about his faith and shared the good news of Jesus Christ with others. As Paul lived out his faith in Jesus Christ, he moved forward, focusing on God's purpose for his life. Paul went through many difficulties and situations that would distract him from his goal; if he hadn't been careful, he could have lost focus on God's purpose for his life.

A few video games have an "open world experience" built into them. The concept of these games is that the player takes control of the main character's life and lives out their life within the game. The main character has a quest that needs to be unveiled as the game proceeds, and it also contains side quests that can be completed. As I play through these games, I am traveling through this open world, completing side quests, and there are so many of them that I can quickly lose focus on the main quest. Like in a video game, our lives can contain side quests that can soon turn our focus away from our primary pursuit.

Paul experienced many "side quests" in his life, but he did not lose focus on his primary goal. Paul looked forward to what was ahead when focused on the eternal. I know that I can quickly lose focus in life and must remember to stay focused on the goal. I am sure you can relate. One "side quest" that can make a person lose focus on the eternal is to focus on our physical bodies.

In 2 Corinthians 4:7, Paul compares our earthly bodies to clay jars. Paul writes, "*We now have this light (the Gospel) shining in our hearts, but we ourselves are like fragile clay jars containing this great treasure. This makes it clear that our great power is from God, not from ourselves*" (NLT). The treasure Paul is speaking of is not a pirate's treasure or even material possessions stashed away under your bed, but a treasure that can only be given to us by God himself. Paul is speaking of a treasure contained in all believers in Jesus, which is the light of the gospel. When a person accepts the gospel, a treasure is deposited into a person's life in the person of the Holy Spirit.

Paul then compares our mortal earthly bodies to jars of clay that now contain the message of the gospel. In Paul's day, clay jars were cheap, breakable, replaceable, and served many purposes. Our bodies may feel inferior and fragile and, like clay jars, are worn from the conditions where they are placed. I know my body feels like it is breaking down as I grow older. Maybe you can relate? On the outside, our bodies are breaking down. But our bodies contain treasure *"to show that the surpassing power belongs to God and not to us."*

Paul continues to describe the conditions that place wear and tear on our bodies as we walk through life, shining the light of the gospel. These conditions can cause a person to lose focus on the eternal. In verses 8–9, Paul continues, *"We are pressed on every side by troubles, but we are not crushed. We are perplexed but not driven to despair. We are hunted down, but never abandoned by God. We get knocked down, but we are not destroyed. Through suffering, our bodies continue to share in the death of Jesus so that the life of Jesus may also be seen in our bodies"* (NLT). Paul's weaknesses apply to everyone who walks by faith and not sight. In those moments when we become pressured, perplexed, persecuted, and even struck down by believing in Jesus Christ, God will never abandon us.

Paul and his companions lived under constant danger of death as they lived out their faith. Paul reminded the Corinthian believers about the difficult situations that they would come up against. Paul writes, *"Yes, we live under constant danger of death because we serve Jesus so that the life of Jesus will be evident in our dying bodies. So, we live in the face of death, which has resulted in eternal life for you. But we continue to preach because we have the same faith the psalmist had when he said, "I believed in God, so I spoke." We know that God, who raised the*

*Lord Jesus, will also raise us with Jesus and present us to himself together with you. All of this is for your benefit. And as God's grace reaches more and more people, there will be great thanksgiving, and God will receive more and more glory. That is why we never give up. Though our bodies are dying, our spirits are renewed every day. For our present troubles are small and won't last very long. Yet they produce for us a glory that vastly outweighs them and will last forever! So, we don't look at the troubles we can see now; rather, **we fix our gaze on things that cannot be seen. For the things we see now will soon be gone, but the things we cannot see will last forever**"* (2 Corinthians 4:11–18 NLT).

Paul kept his focus on the eternal for the benefit of others. When those side quests came into Paul's life, he would use every opportunity to share the saving faith of Jesus with others. When his present troubles would attempt to make him lose focus, Paul reminded himself that these troubles wouldn't last very long. Whether it was his body breaking down, struggling financially, or even health issues, he focused on God by trying to please the Lord.

Walking by Faith Pleases the Lord

Up to this point, we have learned from Paul that walking by faith, not by sight, requires a biblical faith, an eternal purpose, and an eternal focus. Now, Paul will teach us that when we walk by faith, not sight, our ambition should be to please the Lord.

Paul continues in 2 Corinthians 5:6–10, *"So we are always of good courage. We know that while we are at home in the body, we are away from the Lord, for we walk by faith, not by sight. Yes, we are of good courage, and we would rather be away from the body and at home with the Lord. So whether we are at home or away, **we make it our aim to please him**. For we must all appear before the judgment seat of Christ so that each one may receive what is due for what he has done in the body, whether good or evil"* (ESV).

To understand what Paul was speaking about, let's use the analogy of an athlete. Just think about an athlete for a second. An athlete will play home or away games to please their coach. An athlete strongly desires success, winning games, and being a good teammate. Like athletes who want to please the coach, we each want to please someone.

One of my daughters is on the high school swim team. During swim practice one day, she looked at an upcoming swim meet and realized she was not scheduled to swim. She desired to please the coach in past swim competitions by trying her hardest during the meet. But this upcoming swim meet was different. Not being able to swim during the meet would not have bothered her until she realized that the meet was the one that her father could attend. Then, her desire changed. She contacted the coach to see if he could add her to the competition so I could watch her swim. She wanted me to witness her swim, because she wanted to please me by making me proud of her achievements. As we walk through life by faith, our aim should be to please our heavenly Father, just as my daughter wanted to please me by participating in the swim meet.

Paul says that whether he was at a "home game" or an "away game," his goal was to please the Lord in everything he did. The term for aim used in this text is to live a good and pleasing life to God. That should be the same desire to please the Lord in every area of our lives. When we think of the word aim, we may think of an archer aiming an arrow at a target. The archer desires to hit the bull's-eye to obtain the most points possible. That was Paul's greatest desire in life, and he aimed toward this goal. Sometimes he hit the bull's-eye, but most of the time, he missed the mark. We cannot perfectly hit the bull's-eye every time through our strength or desire, but it is the Holy Spirit inside of us that accomplishes what we aim to achieve.

Walking by faith, not by sight, begins and ends with God. God is the one who divinely persuades us to place our trust in Jesus Christ. Once we put our faith in him, the Lord reveals his purpose through Scripture. God's purpose for everyone is to come to saving faith in his Son, Jesus Christ, for the forgiveness of sins. This needs to be our eternal focus. With this eternal focus, a purpose to strive for, and a biblical faith empowering us, Christians aim to please God.

Now that we understand how to walk by faith and not sight, let's look at what it means to walk in the Spirit.

Walking in the Spirit

Galatians 5:25 NLT
"Since we are living by the Spirit, let us follow the Spirit's leading in every part of our lives."

My extended family loves to garden. I would watch as both of my grandmothers would spend time in the garden creating gorgeous flower arrangements within their landscapes. My grandmothers cared for their gardens with great joy, tending to the flowers and giving manicures to the shrubs surrounding them. But tending to the garden went a bit further; they wanted to have lush green lawns that you could run out on barefoot—no sticks, no weeds, just soft green grass that would tickle your toes. My grandparents enjoyed the love of the outdoors while gardening, and my dad followed suit. The love of gardening is a never-ending pursuit of planting, replanting, and adding new additions to a garden that has become part of an evolving landscape. What makes gardening fun is the constant changes that improve the overall garden.

Gardening is not the only area of a person's landscape that can evolve; those with ponds in their yards have another ecosystem that continues to grow. My dad and I added the love of homemade ponds to our love of gardening. As a pond owner, I must say there is nothing as relaxing as sitting by the pond while hearing the water flowing off the waterfalls.

Now, you may ask, what do gardens and ponds have to do with walking in the Spirit? Well, I'm glad you asked. A person who walks with the Spirit will allow the Holy Spirit to lead in every area of their life. The Spirit is tending to your life, molding you into the model of Jesus. As a result, your life will be full of constant changes as the Holy Spirit transforms you into the person you are meant to be.

The process that the Holy Spirit uses in our lives to mold us is called sanctification. Sanctification is a fancy word meaning "the proper state of functioning."

To sanctify someone is to set that person apart for the use intended by its designer. The Greek word translated "sanctification" (*hagiasmos*) means "holiness." To sanctify, therefore, means to make holy. Thus, a human being is sanctified when living according to God's design and purpose.[3]

Gardens and ponds are set apart from the rest of the landscape for the use intended by the designer, the same way as how lives should be lived according to God's design.

When someone accepts Jesus as Lord, the work begins. When God looks at you, he sees the landscape of your life and knows what you will become before you do. The key is allowing the Holy Spirit to guide you through your daily living. "*So, I say, let the Holy Spirit guide your lives,*" says the Apostle Paul (Galatians 5:16 NLT).

When a new believer accepts the Lord Jesus as Savior and Lord, the Holy Spirit comes and lives inside him or her. But for the Holy Spirit to truly guide your life, Jesus's authority must increase and your authority must decrease over your own life. Often, Christians do not fully understand the power of the Holy Spirit inside them, so they are unwilling to allow the Spirit to control every area of their life fully. For the Spirit to work, you must be willing to trust that God has a better plan for you than you do and allow the Spirit to begin work within you, giving him access to every area of your life. If we can better grasp and trust the Holy Spirit's power within us, we will be more willing, as Paul was, to allow the Spirit to control our lives.

Walking in the Spirit Begins with God's Blueprint

When I moved into my home, I had a perfect spot in the backyard to install a pond with a garden around it. The plot of land was unappealing, full of dead grass and hostas, and as I gazed at that area, I imagined what that area could become. I envisioned the pond with its waterfall and the flowing streams around it. I had the shape of the pond in mind, the depth, and even the cost of putting it all together.

When I decided to put a pond in my backyard, I did not wake up one day, strap on my tool belt, and dig. First, I had to read and do research. I watched YouTube videos from some of the seasoned pond-building professionals from around the US. I even went to a class on how to build ponds and water features. When I took the time to learn about building a pond, I understood what was expected of me before I created the pond. I had to realize the cost and the steps needed to maintain the pond throughout the years. Then, I created a blueprint of what the pond would look like, dimensions included.

God not only has a blueprint for Christian living contained within Scripture, but he has an individualized blueprint for your life. The Holy Spirit will act like the pond contractor, following that blueprint until the work is done.

One man thought he had the correct blueprint for his life, and his name was Paul. Paul was later enlightened by God and given a new blueprint to follow for his life. As Paul began to follow God's blueprint, he learned to walk in the Spirit. Today, we are lucky because Paul went on to share the steps he learned about walking in the Spirit.

As believers in Christ, we must know what is expected of us, and ask ourselves, "Are we walking in God's blueprint or our blueprint?" We must learn about these blueprints through the Bible to best obtain the answer. God's Word contains instructions on what is involved in allowing the Holy Spirit to guide us. There are so many instructions that we can only cover a few of them in this chapter, as Paul has outlined. I encourage you to spend time in God's Word daily; only then will you truly come to know God's blueprint for your life.

Walking in the Spirit Will Cost You

Installing a pond can cost a lot of money. Many supplies must be purchased before one can even begin digging the hole. The materials needed to build a pond have a cost, but the cost of time is another factor to consider.

Before you begin construction, you must count the cost of building. Jesus told his disciples in Luke 14:28 NLT that they should not start building without counting the cost. Jesus said, "*But don't begin until you count the cost. For who would begin construction of a building without first calculating the cost to see if there is enough money to finish it?*"

When we allow the Holy Spirit to guide our lives, some costs must be considered. When we spend money, we do so to improve our lives. When the Holy Spirit spends his money to improve our lives, there are also costs, things that we must give up in return. To walk in the Spirit, the price is giving up sinful desires and replacing them with what God desires.

For some, these actions listed here in Paul's letter to the Galatians may seem too costly to give up. But the cost of not giving them up is much higher. Are you willing to give up the One who is wanting to guide you?

The Cost of Walking in Sinful Desires Instead of in the Spirit

In Galatians 5, verses 16–25, the apostle Paul encourages the Christian believers to count the cost they would pay if they allowed their sinful nature to guide them instead of the Holy Spirit.

> "*So, I say, let the Holy Spirit guide your lives. Then you won't be doing what your sinful nature craves. The sinful nature wants to do evil, which is just the opposite of what the Spirit wants.*

And the Spirit gives us desires that are the opposite of what the sinful nature desires. These two forces are constantly fighting each other, so you are not free to carry out your good intentions.

When you follow the desires of your sinful nature, the results are very clear: sexual immorality, impurity, lustful pleasures, idolatry, sorcery, hostility, quarreling, jealousy, outbursts of anger, selfish ambition, dissension, division, envy, drunkenness, wild parties, and other sins like these. Let me tell you again, as I have before, that anyone living that sort of life will not inherit the Kingdom of God" (NLT).

Continuing to walk in sin will cost a person more than they bargained for. The ultimate cost is not inheriting the Kingdom of God. Paul is talking to individuals who may have professed to be Christian but have not received salvation. Since they have not received salvation from their sins, they continue to live according to their sinful desire. When they counted the cost of following Christ, it was not worth it to them to give up what they desired. *"Anyone who continues to live in him will not sin. But anyone who keeps on sinning does not know him or understand who he is"* (1 John 3:6 NLT).

The Cost of Walking with the Spirit Instead of Sinful Desires

When you have counted the cost, you know who Jesus is. You understand the cost and will allow the Holy Spirit to take the blueprint that God has for your life and will allow him to mold you. Paul continues in Galatians 5 verses 22–25 by sharing the positive costs of allowing the Holy Spirit to guide our lives.

"But the Holy Spirit produces this kind of fruit in our lives: love, joy, peace, patience, kindness, goodness, faithfulness, gentleness, and self-control. There is no law against these things! Those who belong to Christ Jesus have nailed the passions and desires of their sinful nature to his cross and crucified them there. Since

we are living by the Spirit, let us follow the Spirit's leading in every part of our lives."

I don't know about you, but I would rather reject the sinful costs and accept the Holy Spirit's costs of having more love and allowing him to produce these godly characteristics in my life. It is better to count the cost of following the Spirit, which leads to eternal life, than to live in sin and not inherit the Kingdom of God in the afterlife.

Let the Building Begin!

Now that we have counted the cost of following Jesus, it's time to let the Holy Spirit produce his work, the work God has for us. Like the pond-building process, once I have all the equipment—the waterfall filter, the pond skimmer, the liner, and even the rocks—I can start to build it. God takes his blueprint for you, your talents and abilities, along with the spiritual gifts that the Holy Spirit produces in your life and begins to create the person you were meant to be. When you allow the Holy Spirit to work in your life, he won't stop until you are completed.

Building a pond is a dirty process. You must have a starting point. For a pond, the starting point is the location on which you will create it. Spiritually speaking, you are the pond, built on the foundation (ground) of Jesus Christ. Now, the Holy Spirit will begin constructing the pieces to form a completed work of art.

The Holy Spirit removes the dirt areas to make room for the beautiful pond. These "dirt areas" in a person's life are the habits of sin and disobedience to God. The Holy Spirit will take the mess of your life and will turn it into a message of hope for others to see. Then, as you continue to walk in the Spirit, allowing him to work in your life, he will put all the pieces together until you are completed.

Walking in the Spirit Requires Daily and Yearly Maintenance

I've been asked if having a pond requires a lot of work. It's not hard work to own a pond. Yes, it took hard work to build the pond, but as the pond evolves, simple maintenance is required. But when people avoid daily care, their pond suffers just as a person's walk with the Spirit becomes vulnerable when care is avoided. Depending on the pond, a person must do daily, weekly, and yearly maintenance. The weekly maintenance would ensure the skimmer is clean to collect more debris that falls into the water. Maintenance requires a check of the system and a filter washdown. Daily or weekly care is quick until you get to the yearly cleaning.

I dread spending an entire two days cleaning the pond every spring as I age. When I winterize the pond, I will go all winter without maintenance and it will freeze over. Under the ice, green string algae forms, and the pond looks slimy and gross by springtime. Around April, when the weather is decent enough to clean the pond, I get my hands dirty.

When I begin, I first must remind myself that the result of deep cleaning the pond will be worth the time spent. Second, I only need to do cleanup once a year. I start by draining some of the water out of the pond. Then, once the pond reaches a certain level, I use the existing water to flush out all the dirt and inhabitants that have settled under the rocks at the bottom of the pond. I take my power washer, spray down around the pond, and continue draining it. Layer by layer, I repeat the process until the rocks are clean and the pond is empty.

When I get to this step, I come to the perfect opportunity to fix areas of the pond that need adjusting. I redo rocks around the stream. I add stones here and there until I get the look that I am trying to achieve. This step is an excellent time to add or evolve an area of the pond that needs improvement.

Just as my pond froze over and grew stagnant over the winter, our Christian walk may experience the same effect. Our lives can become stale, and when we relax, the opportunity for algae buildup can grab on and grow. Being stagnant and not moving forward in the Spirit can cause us to live by the flesh and make a mess out of our lives. We stumble and begin to follow the desires of the flesh. We might compromise here, or a justification over there as to why we started to follow the wishes of the flesh.

When we are in that state of mind, as a believer, the Holy Spirit will not allow us to stay in that pattern of sinful living. When we fall into sinful ways, we need to repent, ask for forgiveness, and let the Holy Spirit clean up the areas of our lives that became contaminated by sin. The Holy Spirit will do a deep cleaning of the areas that have been affected and will power-wash you through discipline.

When the Holy Spirit is allowed to perform daily and weekly maintenance, we can avoid becoming stagnant, and remain clean. We need to stay in constant communion with the Holy Spirit as we walk through life.

Sanctification Is Completed in Christ

The work of sanctification that the Holy Spirt begins in you will continue until completion. Paul writes in Philippians 1:6 NLT, *"And I am certain that God, who began the good work within you, will continue his work until it is finally finished on the day when Christ Jesus returns."* We will be a completed being when we meet Jesus during the rapture, or when we die and enter eternity. Until then, we are to continue to walk in the Spirit. One of the neatest qualities of a Spirit-filled walk is that we walk zealously to please the Lord Jesus Christ.

Walk with Zeal

Acts 22:3 NLT
*"I became very zealous to honor God in everything I did,
just like all of you today."*

As a Christian, I have seen a transformation as I live out my Christian walk. As I grow in the Lord, I am more zealous to please God in everything I do. As a young believer, I was enthusiastic to serve the Lord, but only on Sundays. But as I have grown in my faith, I took baby steps to grow closer to the Lord. For each step I took, I became zealous to serve the Lord seven days a week, three hundred and sixty-five days a year. Maybe you're asking yourself, How did he get to that place where he is zealous for the Lord? If you are at that place of wanting to become zealous to honor God in everything that you do, then you came to the right place. In this chapter, we will look at the apostle Paul's zeal and how he took steps to become zealous to honor the Lord in everything he did.

Before, Paul aimed to please God, but his zealousness was misdirected. After he had met the Lord on the Damascus Road, the Lord redirected his zeal, and the great apostle Paul walked with a new zeal, a righteous zeal. What I admire about Paul is his zealousness to please the Lord. I've wondered how Paul became zealous for the Lord. How did Paul cultivate a zealous behavior to please God? As we study the apostle's life, we will soon learn how to develop a zealousness to please the Lord. But first, let's define what zeal is.

According to Merriam-Webster, zeal is an "eagerness and ardent interest in the pursuit of something."[4] This definition perfectly describes Paul's zeal. We can compare zeal to a pot of water. As the water heats up, it will start to boil. The water does not boil instantly; it is a process that happens over time. If you are not careful, the water can boil over the pan and cause chaos. When a person becomes zealous for what drives them, their passion boils over, and, in a moment, their zeal turns into action. The action produced can sometimes be misdirected or redirected. We will learn from studying Paul's life that he acted on his zeal when misdirected. Paul had moments where he had to have his zeal redirected and times where he had to restrain his zeal.

Examples of Zeal in Action

But before diving into Paul's life, let's look at a few examples of zeal in action in Scripture. The first example that I want to focus on occurs in Numbers 25, and is the story of Phinehas's zeal in action. The story begins with the Israelites being camped at Acacia grove. While stationed there, some men had sexual relations with local Moabite women (women from another nation). This act led these men into the Moabite pagan cult of worshiping a false God, violating the first commandment. In response to their actions, the Lord's zealous anger sent a plague into Israel to punish them for sinning against the Lord. As we read the story of Phinehas, we will see how one man's zealous response will lead to the end of the plague and a commendation from the Lord.

In Numbers 25, verse 2, the Bible records:

> *These women invited (these men) to attend sacrifices to their gods, so the Israelites feasted with them and worshiped the gods of Moab. In this way, Israel joined in the worship of Baal of Peor, causing the Lord's anger to blaze against his people. The Lord issued the following command to Moses: "Seize all the ringleaders and execute them before the Lord in broad*

daylight, so his fierce anger will turn away from the people of Israel." So, Moses ordered Israel's judges, "Each of you must put to death the men under your authority who have joined in worshiping Baal of Peor." Just then, one of the Israelite men brought a Midianite woman into his tent, right before the eyes of Moses and all the people, as everyone was weeping at the entrance of the Tabernacle. When Phinehas, son of Eleazar and grandson of Aaron, the priest, saw this, he jumped up and left the assembly. He took a spear and rushed after the man into his tent. Phinehas thrust the spear all the way through the man's body and into the woman's stomach (Numbers 25:2–8 NLT).

Phinehas had heard what the Lord God had commanded Moses on how to respond to this injustice. Phinehas was zealous for the Lord and acted by following the Lord's commands, and because of Phinehas's action, the Lord replied to Moses. He said:

*Phinehas, son of Eleazar and grandson of Aaron, the priest, has turned my anger away from the Israelites by being as zealous among them as I was. So, I stopped destroying all Israel as I had intended to do in my zealous anger. Now tell him that I am making my special covenant of peace with him. In this covenant, I give him and his descendants a permanent right to the priesthood, for **in his zeal for me, his God,** he purified the people of Israel, making them right with me* (Numbers 25:11–13 NLT).

A second example is from the life of King Saul. 2 Samuel 21:1–2 records the result of Saul's zeal:

There was a famine during David's reign that lasted for three years, so David asked the Lord about it. And the Lord said, "The famine has come because Saul and his family are guilty of murdering the Gibeonites." So, the king summoned the Gibeonites. They were not part of Israel but were all that was *left of the nation of the Amorites. The people of Israel had sworn not to kill them, **but Saul, in his zeal for Israel and Judah, had tried to wipe them out***" (NLT).

Phinehas acted with zeal in obedience to the Lord, whereas Saul acted in disobedience to God. Two individuals were as zealous as God in pursuing holiness and justice. Saul's zeal was misdirected because he acted in disobedience toward God.

Misdirected Zeal

Saul was not the only one who had a zeal that was misdirected. In Paul's letter to the Galatians, Paul told the believers about his former lifestyle in Judaism. Paul writes, "*For you have heard of my former life in Judaism, how I persecuted the church of God violently and tried to destroy it. And I was advancing in Judaism beyond many of my own age among my people, so extremely zealous was I for the traditions of my fathers*" (Galatians 1:13–14 ESV). Paul was so zealous about obeying the law that he tried to stop anything that stood against it. Paul took his zeal to the extreme. He became so focused on observing the law and his fore-fathers' traditions that his zealous passion closed his eyes to the truth.

In Paul's words, he:

> *Persecuted the followers of the way, hounding some to death, arresting both men and women and throwing them in prison. The high priest and the whole council of elders can testify that this is so. For I received letters from them to our Jewish brothers in Damascus, authorizing me to bring the followers of the way from there to Jerusalem, in chains, to be punished* (Acts 22: 4–5).

And he was "*so zealous that I harshly persecuted the church. And as for righteousness, I obeyed the law without fault*" (Philippians 3:6).

Later in the first century, Jewish historian Josephus recorded a class of men, Zealots, who rigorously adhered to the Mosaic law. They endeavored even by resorting to violence, following the example of Phinehas, to prevent religion from being violated by others. Still, in the latter days of the Jewish commonwealth, they used their misplaced holy zeal as a pretext for evil.[5] The zealots misinterpreted God's Word. When they read the story of Phinehas, they missed the whole purpose of why the story was recorded in the Scriptures. The purpose was that Phinehas demonstrated zeal to obey the Lord in that specific moment for a particular purpose.

Both examples are of those who are deeply committed to keeping religion or misinterpreted the Scriptures, and their zeal became misdirected toward the wrong reasons. Walking with zeal for God is not a natural byproduct of human effort. Zeal must first be cultivated within an individual before being acted upon.

Cultivating Zeal

Paul did not automatically have a zeal for his pursuits in life. Paul's enthusiasm for Judaism and for spreading the gospel was cultivated throughout his lifetime, beginning at a young age as Paul would come face-to-face with people in authority who challenged his zeal for serving God. Paul would give his testimony, and he would start at the beginning.

There was a time when Paul got arrested in the Temple for preaching the gospel. Paul was once detained by Lysias, a high-ranking Roman official (Acts 23:6) who thought that Paul was a criminal that they were looking for. When questioned, Paul responded with his testimony. Acts 22:3–5 records, "*Then Paul said, 'I am a Jew, born in Tarsus, a city in Cilicia, and I was brought up and educated here in Jerusalem under Gamaliel. As his student, I was carefully trained in our Jewish laws and customs. I became very zealous to honor God in everything I did, just like all of you today.'*"

Later in life, Paul stood before king Agrippa when he was arrested again. Once again, Paul testified and said, "*I was given a thorough Jewish training from my earliest childhood among my own people and in Jerusalem. If they would admit it, they know that I have been a member of the Pharisees, the strictest sect of our religion.*"

In his letter to the Philippians, Paul describes his lofty achievements as a Jew and his upbringing. Philippians 3:5–6 records Paul's words: "*I was circumcised when I was eight days old. I am a pure-blooded citizen of Israel and a member of the tribe of Benjamin—a real Hebrew if there ever was one! I was a member of the Pharisees, who demand the strictest obedience to the Jewish law.*"

Paul grew up and was educated from a young age under the training of Gamaliel. Not only was he educated, but he was carefully trained in Jewish laws and customs. Paul spent time with this religious man and grew to interpret the Scriptures as he cultivated a zeal to obey God and to honor him with everything he did.

To cultivate a zeal for the Lord as Paul did, we must first spend time with other believers and learn within a church community. Paul would go into the Temple daily and be trained with other believers. Paul would socialize with other believers as he grew in his faith. Just as the Temple was a place to worship God in the first century, the church today is a place to go and worship God with like-minded believers. If you are not in the habit of attending church, then take that step to attend often. Start small and go every Sunday; if your church offers a Sunday or Wednesday night church service, you can join in those as well. Just ensure you do not just arrive at the beginning and leave at the end without getting to know someone.

Paul was not the only one at that time being trained by Gamaliel. Paul was a part of a group of students who all were learning together. Paul stated this himself when he told the churches in Galatia that he "*was advancing in Judaism beyond many of my own age among my people, so extremely zealous was I for the traditions of my fathers*" (Galatians 1:14). The second baby step for cultivating zeal is to spend time with seasoned believers. These seasoned believers can be pastors, well-trained teachers, or elders. Another method is to join a small group. In a small group, Christians meet weekly to grow in their walk with Christ and be strengthened. In a small group, Christians interact with other believers as they spend time in God's Word and unpack what God wants them to learn from him. When you join a small group and join in fellowship, you will be challenged as you grow together and have your faith strengthened. Another benefit of joining a small group is that your prayer life will be maintained. When you pray for the other believers in your group, and they pray for you, your focus will be on each other's needs. You will be there to support and comfort you in your time of need.

As Paul was being trained in the Temple, he had to discipline himself. Paul had to become disciplined to spend time in God's Word and an allotted time for dedicated prayer. Our third baby step is to spend time in the Scriptures daily, learning from God through the Holy Spirit. By spending time in God's Word, the Holy Spirit will grow us in wisdom and knowledge and will generate excitement from within to grow and become zealous for the Lord. Start small, if you are not in the habit of spending time in prayer and God's Word. Begin by reading God's Word for 15 minutes a day. Spend 15 minutes in prayer to God daily. Then, finally, share with someone for 15 minutes what you have learned. As you interact with the Lord with these small steps, the Lord will move and speak into your life. Over time, you will desire to spend more than 15 minutes with him.

Zeal is cultivated by seeking God, spending time learning from and being mentored by seasoned believers in a church community, cultivating relationships and prayer by being part of a small group, and by spending time daily in scripture and in prayer. Through these simple steps we can become more zealous to serve the Lord in everything we do.

Walking through the Storm

It was a warm evening here in Minnesota, and the weather was primed to be severe. A severe thunderstorm warning was issued for our county, and the sirens began to go off. My daughter and I were already in the basement, unaware of the severe weather, until my wife and other daughters came downstairs. Our phones went off with a warning telling us to go downstairs and take cover because of tornados. Suddenly, the power went off. Outside, the night sky was lit with massive lightning strikes, bellowing thunder, and wicked wind. We had experienced storms like this before and knew what steps to take during the storm to remain safe.

However, I love to watch storms pass through. Something about watching a storm invigorates me, at least from a distance. One year, a tornado was going down the road in a city next to mine, and our house was exactly two miles away from the tornado's path. I sat by my deck and had never seen the wind whip so much. I watched as my patio set got blown from one end of the deck to the other. I was in the middle of a storm, closer than ever to a tornado. Once the storm passed, there was damage to homes and to many trees that could not stand up to the wind. Luckily, the damage was minor, and we safely escaped it. We can experience many storms that are not severe weather, but the kinds that come in trials, suffering, and tribulation. I have heard it said that people either are entering a storm, are amid it, or have exited it. In these storms, we can sometimes experience loss or even get damaged, but how we respond during and after these storms will make a difference.

If there is anybody in Scripture who went through many storms in life, it is the apostle Paul. In Paul's second letter to the Corinthian church, contained within the Bible, he mentioned the trials he experienced in life to the congregation. In II Corinthians 11: 23–27, Paul says he has"

> *been put in prison more often, been whipped times without number, and faced death again and again. Five different times the Jewish leaders gave me thirty-nine lashes. Three times I was beaten with rods. Once, I was stoned. Three times I was shipwrecked. Once I spent a whole night and a day adrift at sea. I have traveled on many long journeys. I have faced danger from rivers and from robbers. I have faced danger from my own people, the Jews, as well as from the Gentiles. I have faced danger in the cities, in the deserts, and on the seas. And I have faced danger from men who claim to be believers but are not. I have worked hard and long, enduring many sleepless nights. I have been hungry and thirsty and have often gone without food. I have shivered in the cold, without enough clothing to keep me warm (NLT).*

He talks about going through very difficult trials, the severe storms in his life, and he lived to tell about them. But Paul's trials didn't end there. They continued, even after he penned this letter. As Paul was making his final journey to Rome, we pick up his story as he was about to enter another storm.

Every Storm Has a Beginning

The weather forecaster came on the evening news and issued a weather warning as Minnesota was experiencing its snowiest winter in the last 50 years. Travel would be rough and was not advised. Roads would be icy, with blowing snow and blizzard-like conditions. The weather conditions closed schools, and any workers who could work from home did, except for the frontline workers and others who could not work from home.

The storm was forecasted in the days leading up to the storm. Everyone who knew the storm was coming was told to prepare as the storm approached. I got into my truck the first morning of the storm and headed to work. I knew about the storm, and even though the storm was coming, I had no choice but to enter the storm. I work in a retail environment, and being a store manager, I had no choice but to drive to work so I could open the store.

Similarly, the apostle Paul found himself a prisoner on a ship headed toward Rome when the seas became rough. It was not the correct time of year to be out at sea. Paul perceived that the weather conditions were unfavorable to travel and approached the ship's captain and crew. *"'Men,' he said, 'I believe there is trouble ahead if we go on—shipwreck, loss of cargo, and danger to our lives as well.' But the officer in charge of the prisoners listened more to the ship's captain and the owner than to Paul"* (Acts 27:10–11 NLT). When I was headed to work that day, my boss the night before was contemplating closing the store when she heard the weather report. But instead of heeding the warning, the store would open and resume business as usual. Like the apostle Paul, at times we won't have a choice but to enter a storm.

As the ship continued to sail toward a nearby harbor to overwinter, the winds became so strong that the boat was in danger of sinking. The crew bound a rope around the ship's hull to help keep it intact and tossed their cargo overboard, and *"the terrible storm raged for many days, blotting out the sun and the stars, until at last all hope was gone"* (Acts 27:20 NLT).

Every Storm Has a Middle

In January 2023, Minnesota had the most snowfall recorded since 1992 during a three-day snow event. Then another snowstorm came, and not only did we get a bunch of snow, but we also had falling temperatures, which caused the roads to be icy and slippery. What I do not like about these events is having to drive in them. In the past, I haven't had much luck while driving on slippery roads. There were a few times when my vehicle spun out, and I did a bit of damage to my car, but luckily not to anything or anyone else. So when this weather event occurred, I was white-knuckle driving to work, praying for safety and protection.

The storm raged on when we last left Paul, and the crew had lost all hope. These experienced seamen knew the storm was so bad they would all perish at sea. The book of Acts records that:

> no one had eaten for a long time. Finally, Paul called the crew together and said, "Men, you should have listened to me in the first place and not left Crete. You would have avoided all this damage and loss. But take courage! None of you will lose your lives, even though the ship will go down. For last night, an angel of the God to whom I belong and whom I serve stood beside me, and he said, 'Don't be afraid, Paul, for you will surely stand trial before Caesar! What's more, God in his goodness has granted safety to everyone sailing with you.' So take courage! For I believe God. It will be just as he said" (Acts 27:21–25 NLT).

I compare these weather events to storms that occur that we have no control over. Storms where we must lean on our faith in God to get us through. As I am cautiously driving to work, I am reminded of another storm that Paul went through. Paul and Silas were imprisoned unjustly under false accusations. Not only were they falsely accused, but they were severely beaten. Then the Bible says in Acts 16:25–26, "*Around midnight Paul and Silas were praying and singing hymns to God, and the other prisoners were listening. Suddenly, there was a massive earthquake, and the prison was shaken to its foundations. All the doors immediately flew open, and the chains of every prisoner fell off!"*

Paul and Silas found themselves in the middle of a storm. Paul had a few options. He could have been angry at God for allowing this to happen to them. Paul could have spoken hatefully toward the guards who beat him or made a scene for being wrongly accused. Paul and Silas did not do any of those things. Instead, they sang praises to God.

As my white-knuckle driving continued, praise and worship songs came on the radio, and I began to praise God. As I was singing, I wondered what songs Paul would have sung that night to the Lord. Whatever hymns they were singing pleased the Lord and the other prisoners intently listening. While singing to the Lord, my fear of driving through the storm changed to thanks. Singing praise and worship songs helps me reflect on the goodness of God and that God is in control. I would rather be in a storm with Jesus than go through one without him. Take courage, for the Lord will be with you during the storm.

Every Storm Comes to an End

The one thing familiar with all storms is that every storm has a beginning, a middle, and an end. Winter storms will soon end, and spring rain will begin. The same can be said for any trial, difficulty, and circumstance that comes on us. For the apostle Paul, his storm was about ready to end. The angel of the Lord that had visited Paul on the ship told Paul that the crew and everyone on it would survive the shipwreck that was about to take place. Paul believed in the word of the Lord. He convinced the sailors to stay on board and told them that the Lord ensured everyone's safe arrival on shore.

They began to lose hope once the sailor lost hope due to their circumstances. But now, everyone on board found hope in the Lord because of Paul's actions during the weather event. As we have seen in Paul's life, he believed the word of the Lord during the storms that he found himself in. Next time you find yourself at the beginning of a storm, remember that God will be with you throughout your storm. Lean into him and his word, and God will see you through. The Lord "will be a booth for shade by day from the heat, and for a refuge and a shelter from the storm and rain" (Isaiah 4:6 ESV).

Walk with Joy

Philippians 2:2 ESV
"Complete my joy by being of the same mind, having the same love, being in full accord and of one mind."

Hebrews 12 tells us that Jesus endured the cross because of the joy set before him. Now, you may ask, what was the joy set before him? The new living translation phrases Hebrews 12:2 this way: "*Because of the joy awaiting him, he endured the cross.*" The joy awaiting Jesus is when individuals place their faith in him as Savior and Lord and become children of God. Here is a question for us to consider. Since the joy awaiting Jesus is us, what is the joy we are waiting for? Are we finding joy in knowing Jesus, living for him, and teaching others how to live for Christ? Or are we finding joy in the things of this world that are only temporary?

Joy Is Found in Jesus Christ, Not Found in Our Accomplishments

Paul found joy in getting to know Jesus on a deeper level and he lived for him. On his journey, Paul desired that others who met the Lord would also find joy in living a godly life. Paul came to realize that the joy of the Lord became his strength to survive difficult situations. So much so that Paul, filled with joy while in prison, wrote a letter to the church in Philippi. You read that right: Paul experienced joy while in prison. Paul's joy did not come from his present circumstance but from the joy awaiting him. What was that joy awaiting Paul, that he could experience joy in a difficult circumstance? Paul's joy was twofold. Paul found joy in living for Jesus while teaching fellow believers to do the same. But before Paul could relay to the church why he had this type of joy, he first explained the joy he experienced before meeting Jesus Christ.

Paul had gained a lot of prestige before he became a Christian. He begins to explain to the church why he could place a lot of confidence in his flesh because of his accomplishments. Those accomplishments brought joy to the apostle. Paul was a "Hebrew of Hebrews" who obeyed the law, a Pharisee, and a zealous church persecutor. Paul viewed himself as blameless and self-righteous under the law (Philippians 2:4–6). Do you remember where you placed or found your joy in life before you met Christ? Before Paul met Christ, he thought he had it all. Paul's joy was found in his prestige as a righteous Pharisee and his accomplishments in Judaism, until he met Jesus.

Paul reflected on his accomplishments, which did not compare to the joy of knowing Jesus as Savior and Lord. In his own words, Paul said:

> *But whatever gain I had, I counted as loss for the sake of Christ. Indeed, I count everything as a loss because of the surpassing worth of knowing Christ Jesus, my Lord. For his sake, I have suffered the loss of all things and count them as rubbish, so that I may gain Christ and be found in him, not having a righteousness of my own that comes from the law, but that which comes through faith in Christ, the righteousness from God that depends on faith— that I may know him and the power of his resurrection, and may share his sufferings, becoming like him in his death, that by any means possible I may attain the resurrection from the dead* (Philippians 3:7–11).

You may be asking yourself, Why did Paul convey his desire to know the Lord and to count everything he gained as rubbish? Paul wanted the Philippian church to experience the same joy that Paul experienced by knowing Jesus. Paul viewed the believers at the church in

Philippi as his children. Just as a parent can experience joy when they see their children mature, Paul experienced that same joy when fellow believers developed their relationship with Jesus. When Paul witnessed his church in Philippi growing in their faith, he knew they were getting to know Jesus on a deeper level.

Joy Is Found in Partnership and Prayer

In Philippians 1, Paul joyfully made prayer requests for the believers in Philippi. The church became Paul's partner in spreading the good news of Christ from the first time they heard the message (Philippians 1:3–5). Paul would continually pray for the believers that they would find joy when they shared their faith in the gospel. As Christians, we should follow Paul's example as we pray for the church we attend. Being a part of a church means that Christians become partners with other believers in spreading the good news, just as the Philippian church did. We need to offer prayers for other believers to stand firm and support each other as we continue the mission that God gave to the church. Christians can experience great joy when they partner with other Christians to share the gospel message because the gospel brings joy with it. Those who have joy must expect to go through hard work before experiencing the joy of the harvest.

Partnering with other believers in sharing the gospel means that we defend and confirm the truth of the good news (Philippians 1:7). When you read the words for defense and confirmation in the Greek text, you can better understand what Paul was relaying to the church. The Greek word for "defense" is *apologia*; we get our word apologetics from it. Apologetics means making a verbal defense of the Scriptures as to why one believes the Scriptures are true. The Philippian church defended their faith with a well-reasoned reply. The Greek word that Paul uses for "confirmation" is *bebaiosis*. This word means to be confident in what you believe. Paul and the Philippian church were confident in the word of God. Paul was communicating to the church that he found joy in hearing that they were partnering with him through making verbal, well-reasoned replies for why they believed in Jesus Christ and the Scriptures.

Peter tells us in 1 Peter 3:15, *"Always be prepared to give an answer to everyone who asks you to give the reason for the hope that you have. But do this with gentleness and respect"* (NIV). How do you get prepared to answer the hope that you have? That is one of those questions that will take a lifetime of continuous learning and sharing. Paul had spent many years learning about Judaism and three years with Jesus Christ in Arabia before he went full-time into ministry to share the gospel with Jews and Gentiles. The key takeaway is that properly defending why you believe in the gospel takes time, effort, and a good teacher. You can gain confidence in the Scriptures by reading God's Word and praying with other believers. But it also comes from exercising your faith in Jesus Christ. Paul began to exercise his faith by first going into the synagogues to share the good news of Jesus.

His mission was to persuade the Jews to believe in the message of Jesus. Paul would attempt to persuade the Jews by verbalizing a well-reasoned response as to why they should believe that Jesus Christ is the Messiah. Paul's joy came from fulfilling the calling that Jesus gave him. I can relate to this when I share my testimony with someone about the unexplainable things that have happened in my life. Those God moments make me smile with inexpressible joy when God is the only explanation. Joy and confidence are not hard to come by. When we live for Christ, our joy comes from the Father's joy.

Joy Is Found When You Live a Life for Christ

Joy can be found in prayer, partnership, and living for Christ. In his Philippian letter, Paul continues to address the church by encouraging them to develop in a few areas in order to grow in joy and unity. Paul desires all believers to find joy in living for Christ. But to do that, the believers would have to continue to grow in these four areas. These same areas in a believer's life that Paul addressed to the Philippian church are the same areas all believers need to grow even today.

The believers had to:

1) Keep growing in the knowledge and understanding of the Lord and his ways (1:9).

2) Have a love for Christ and others that overflows more and more (1:9).

3) Understand what matters so they may live pure and blameless lives for the Lord (1:10).

4) Live a life filled with the fruit of righteousness through Jesus Christ (1:11).

The first area is to keep growing in the knowledge and understanding of the Lord and his ways. What practical ways can believers continue to grow and understand the Lord today? The most important thing is to spend quiet time with Jesus by reading God's Word. The Bible is God's revelation to us. God has not kept that hidden. His Word had been written down generations ago teaching us how to grow in the knowledge and understanding of the Lord and his ways. We need to spend time in God's Word daily. Yet, this is the most challenging area in most Christian lives. During our day, life seems to be filled with busyness instead of the proper perspective of seeking after God. In Paul's prayer for the believers, he prayed that they would continue to grow in the Lord. Take that same prayer and make it your own. Pray that God will give you the discipline to spend time in God's Word and open your heart and mind to grow in the knowledge and understanding of the Lord and his ways. I did that at the start of the new year. I took a Bible verse in Exodus 33:13, where Moses asked the Lord for the same prayer, and I made it my own. The prayer goes like this, *"Now therefore, I pray, if I have found grace in Your sight, show me now Your way, that I may know You and that I may find grace in Your sight"* (NKJV).

The second area is a love for Christ and others that overflows more. What practical steps can a believer take today to have a love that overflows? I could spend a whole chapter on how to love the Lord and others, but for this point, let's listen to what Jesus said in Matthew 22:38–39: *"You must love the Lord your God with all your heart, all your soul, and all your mind. This is the first and greatest commandment. A second is equally important: 'Love your neighbor as yourself'"* (NLT). The key takeaway is that joy is found when you love the Lord your God with every part of your being. When you begin loving the Lord as you should, your love for others will overflow with joy.

The third growth area is understanding what matters to live a pure and blameless life for the Lord. What are some things that matter in life? Family matters, work matters, health matters, sleep matters, loving others matters, and so on. However, understanding the first two areas Paul speaks about is foundational. When you seek to know God, his ways, and his commands by spending time in the Bible, you will grow to understand God. When you know God's ways and that he wants what's best for you, you will obey God out of love for him. When you obey God's commands out of a place of love, your love will overflow with others. As you live a life obedient to God, the Holy Spirit will give you the capacity to live purely and blamelessly for the Lord in every area of your life.

The fourth area of growth is to live a life filled with the fruit that living a righteous life produces through Jesus Christ. The Christian life is impossible to live on our own. We can't live a pure and blameless life for Christ in our own strength; we need the power of God's Holy Spirit. When we obey God's Word, the Holy Spirit will produce the fruit of his righteousness that grows within us. This righteous fruit, that Paul is speaking about here, is referred to in Scripture as the fruit of the Spirit (Galatians 5:22–23). The fruit of joy is reflected in the spiritual attitudes and actions characterized by Spirit-led believers. Having both a righteous attitude and righteous actions produces joy and are expressed in displaying acts of kindness toward others. When a believer displays acts of righteousness, those actions are stored up as treasures in heaven (Philippians 4:16–17).

Joy Is Completed in Unity

Paul writes:

> So if there is any encouragement in Christ, any comfort from love, any participation in the Spirit, any affection and sympathy, complete my joy by being of the same mind, having the same love, being in full accord and of one mind. Do nothing from selfish ambition or conceit but in humility count others more significant than yourselves. Let each of you look not only to his own interests, but also to the interests of others. Have this mind among yourselves, which is yours in Christ Jesus, who, though he was in the form of God, did not count equality with God a thing to be grasped, but emptied himself, by taking the form of a servant, being born in the likeness of men. And being found in human form, he humbled himself by becoming obedient to the point of death, even death on a cross. Therefore, God has highly exalted him and bestowed on him the name that is above every name, so that at the name of Jesus every knee should bow, in heaven and on earth and under the earth, and every tongue confess that Jesus Christ is Lord, to the glory of God the Father (Philippians 2:1–11 ESV).

There is a joy that comes from being in unity with other believers. I have experienced joy when I am united with other believers in a small group and when I meet with a group of men every Friday night in a small online group. What brings joy is being able to come along-side others and be honest about the struggles and blessings of living a Christian life. Being united in harmony with others by being in com-munity is what the apostle Paul had in mind when he wrote to the

Philippian church. Paul knew that his joy would be complete when the church would be united *"by being of the same mind, having the same love, being in full accord and of one mind"* (Philippians 2:2). In my small group, we come together with the same mind, focused on Jesus Christ, his word, the great commission, and to live out our faith together. We have the same love for each other and the church. Our love extends to our families and other believers in the faith and those who are lost and need to hear about the good news of Jesus Christ. Being in full accord and of one mind brings joy when we fellowship with Jesus Christ and each other while living in obedience, awaiting the ultimate joy of meeting Christ in heaven. The joy that can be experienced by fellowship with Jesus is a by-product of living a life pleasing to God.

As Christians, we need the joy found in knowing Christ and the joy that comes from being united with each other. When the storms of life come toward us, we will need this support system to help get through these storms. When they come, James tells us to *"count it all joy, my brothers, when you meet trials of various kinds, for you know that the testing of your faith produces steadfastness. And let steadfastness have its full effect, that you may be perfect and complete, lacking in nothing"* (James 1:2–4 ESV).

Walk to Finish Well

Acts 20:24 NLT
"But my life is worth nothing to me unless I use it for finishing the work assigned me by the Lord Jesus—the work of telling others the Good News about the wonderful grace of God."

If the apostle Paul were still alive today and conversing with you, a Christian, he would ask this question, "How are you doing with running your race for Christ?" If you are young, Paul will remind you that life will go by faster than you think and that you should seek out what specific plan the Lord has for you. Once you find it, set your goal to finish well. If you are middle-aged, Paul would ask you to pass the baton of faith onto your children, coworkers, and friends. If you are elderly, Paul will ask you to stay on the course, finish well, and consider the legacy you have passed on to your children, grandchildren, and others.

Paul lived his life to finish well by finishing the work the Lord assigned him. Toward the end of Paul's life, he knew that his race was coming to a close. Paul fought the good fight; he finished his race by keeping the faith (2 Timothy 4:7), and he wanted Timothy, whom he mentored in the gospel of Christ, to finish his race well, too.

The three Greek verbs Paul uses when he says, "I have fought, I have finished, and I have kept," indicate a completed action with continuing results. The results of Paul's ministry continued through Timothy, and the rest of his students, even after Paul had gone. By God's power, Paul accomplished everything God called him to do. Now it was time for Paul to encourage and empower Timothy to do the same. Paul's advice to Timothy was good advice on how to run the race and finish well. No matter where you find yourself on this spiritual journey, young, old, or in between, it doesn't matter when you begin your race for Christ. It is how you finish the race of life that matters.

In Paul's final letter to Timothy, Paul advised his young apprentice to run his race for Christ. Paul encouraged Timothy to always be sober-minded, to endure suffering, to do the work of an evangelist, and to fulfill his ministry (2 Timothy 4:5). When we personalize these four goals that Paul gave Timothy, we can also learn how to finish our race for Christ well.

Finish Well by Staying Sober-Minded

What comes to mind when you think of the word "sober-minded"? When a person is sober, they are not intoxicated. When we think of someone who is intoxicated, we think of a drunk person, who has consumed too much wine or alcohol. When intoxicated, a person makes poor decisions and usually feels sick to their stomach by the next day. When I hear someone state that they are drug- and alcohol-free, I am impressed that they had the discipline to make choices that would keep them from becoming impaired. They want to remain clear-headed so that they can make proper decisions. As Peter says in 1 Peter 1:13, those individuals prepare their minds for action. By being sober-minded, they do not become intoxicated with the various allurements of this world that would tempt them to make poor choices.

If we are not careful, the allurements of this world can quickly intoxicate us. They can easily distract us from our priorities as believers in Jesus Christ. Paul is telling Timothy to train his mind and always keep it in check so the actions of his hands, eyes, and thoughts will not distract from focusing on the priorities of the faith. As Paul ran his race, he preserved the integrity of his ministry and the Christian faith, because he did not want to be disqualified. Paul told the Corinthian church that he had to train his mind to stay sober-minded. *"I discipline my body like an athlete, training it to do what it should. Otherwise, I fear that after preaching to others, I myself might be disqualified"* (1 Corinthians 9:27 NLT).

What does being sober-minded as a Christian mean, and why is it necessary to finish well? The apostles Paul and Peter both mention that we prepare our minds, and Peter tells us to *"prepare your minds for action and exercise self-control"* (1 Peter 1:13).

1. Being Sober-Minded Begins with Training

Paul wanted Timothy to learn from him and continue to train like an athlete. Training one's body as an athlete begins with the mind. A person must consciously decide to spend time working out at the gym. The decision to eat well and not allow contaminants to enter the body is also essential to working out and training well. A man who qualified for the Ironman World Championship in Finland during the summer of 2023 had to work very hard to qualify. He had to strive to be one of the best in the entire world to participate in the event. For the previous few years, he had been putting in the hard work training his body by doing exhausting bike rides, swimming beside boats on the lake, etc., to become the best. He was constantly preparing his body. His goals were to compete and strive to win while competing with the world's best.

Just as Paul told the Corinthians, *"Don't you realize that in a race everyone runs, but only one person gets the prize? So run to win!"* (1 Corinthians 9:24 NLT).

Training your body and mind is a lifelong sprint to the finish. Not only did this athlete train his body and mind, but he was also disciplined enough to prevent outside distractions from derailing him from his goal. He was so focused that he did not tell anyone in his family that he was training or that he qualified for the Ironman World Championship, to the dismay of his family. They did not understand why he did not tell them. To him, training and qualifying for the tournament did not concern them, even though they wished they had known so they could cheer for him. Sometimes, even those with the best intentions can become intoxicating to an athlete. If only we could be as focused on being sober-minded with our spiritual goals in mind as he was.

2. Training to Become Sober-Minded Leads to Action

An athlete does not train so that he can sit on the sidelines. He prepares to participate in the event. The same focus needs to be implemented when training our minds and bodies for our spiritual race. We train so we can participate and to win the race that God has set before us. What does training your spiritual mind look like when Paul asks us to become sober-minded?

3. Train Yourself to Be Watchful

Peter tells us, "*Be sober-minded; be watchful. Your adversary, the devil, prowls around like a roaring lion, seeking someone to devour*" (1 Peter 5:8 ESV).

The devil can use things to intoxicate you. His goal is to distract you from running your race and to take your focus off what God wants you to accomplish. Have you ever considered how the devil can intoxicate you? Intoxicants can include success, pride, financial gain, self-centeredness, lack of motivation, distractions, material gain, or anything that will lure you away from God. The devil wants you to become distracted and will look for ways to overwhelm the believer into giving up. Don't give up! Keep training so you can stay alert and watchful.

4. Train Every Part of Who You Are to Be Sober-Minded

Paul told Titus to teach every believer sound doctrine. It did not matter if they were older or younger believers; he needed to train them all. Paul writes:

Teach the older men to exercise self-control, to be worthy of respect, and to live wisely. They must have sound faith and be filled with love and patience. Similarly, teach the older women to live in a way that honors God. They must not slander others or be heavy drinkers. Instead, they should teach others what is good. These older women must train the younger women to love their husbands and their children, to live wisely and be pure, to work in their homes, to do good, and to be submissive to their husbands. Then they will not bring shame on the word of God. In the same way, encourage the young men to live wisely. And you yourself must be an example to them by doing good works of every kind. Let everything you do reflect the integrity and seriousness of your teaching. Teach the truth so that your teaching can't be criticized. Then those who oppose us will be ashamed and have nothing bad to say about us (Titus 2:2–8 NLT).

5. Train to Be Ready for Action

Paul told the church in 1 Thessalonians 5:6 to always be on their guard, stay alert, and stay sober in this life as we await Christ's return. When we use our training to further God's ministry for us, an attitude of joy accompanies any sacrificial Christian service—more on that as we work through this chapter.

Finish Well by Enduring Suffering

What if the apostle Paul came up to you and told you that, as Christians, we are destined for affliction because we believe in Jesus Christ? He goes on to say to you that you may experience suffering and persecution for making a stand for Christ. How would you respond? Would you be encouraged or scared? Would the emotions of nervousness concerning the future bring you discomfort? Or would you take comfort in the realization that you may experience affliction and choose to rejoice because you are now a Christian? Paul wrote about suffering for Christ and the gospel in many of his letters in the New Testament. Paul experienced suffering and forewarned new Christians that suffering for the cause of Christ is a part of the Christian experience.

Now that Paul encouraged Timothy to be sober-minded, he is encouraging him to endure suffering. Suffering is one of the greatest allurements the devil will use to turn someone away from God. Think back to our athlete. He decides to train his body to participate in the Ironman competition. Then, he decides to begin to prepare. As he trains, his body suffers as he is breaking down muscle to build it up and strengthen it. You have probably heard "no pain, no gain" before. It is a phrase used in gyms to motivate someone to endure muscle pain to become stronger or healthier.

1. Enduring Suffering Brings Comfort

Sounds like an oxymoron. Why would enduring suffering bring comfort? Paul told the church in Corinth:

> *Blessed be the God and Father of our Lord Jesus Christ, the Father of mercies and God of all comfort, who comforts us in all our affliction, so that we may be able to comfort those who are in any affliction, with the comfort with which we ourselves are comforted by God. For as we share abundantly in Christ's sufferings, so through Christ we share abundantly in comfort too. If we are afflicted, it is for your comfort and salvation; and if we are comforted, it is for your comfort, which you experience when you patiently endure the same sufferings that we suffer. Our hope for you is unshaken, for we know that as you share in our sufferings, you will also share in our comfort* (2 Corinthians 1:3–7).

Paul told Timothy that suffering comes when you work in God's workout gym. But in the end, the suffering will lead to a reward. Let's face it; no one likes to suffer physically or mentally unless there is a reward. Working toward the satisfaction of receiving the prize is what brings comfort. Suffering does not happen alone but happens to all Christians. When we understand that we suffer together, it should comfort us that we are not alone.

2. We Endure Suffering Because of Our Choice to Follow Christ

To finish well for Christ, be prepared to experience some suffering. Suffering can come from rejection from your coworkers or being disowned by those closest to you. Close friends can become distant, and relationships can become strained when those around you do not know Christ. They see you as someone who has changed, so they shy away because they cannot relate to your new relationship with the Lord. Once I graduated from Grace Christian University with my pastoral degree, I announced that I decided to pursue the calling that God laid upon me to be a pastor. At once, I had close family embrace me and a few who questioned my decision. I had close friends who suddenly backed away and a few pushbacks. Even when I launched my podcast and website, I received both positive and negative comments. But the negative responses from those I thought were close friends caused me to suffer grief.

When the apostle Paul became a Christian, he probably had other Pharisee friends who rejected him and pushed him away. Then, when he approached other believers in Jerusalem and attempted to join the other disciples, some were afraid and did not believe he had become a Christian. Rejected and pushed away by man but chosen by God to spread the good news to all, Paul experienced emotional suffering for choosing to obey and pursue the life God commanded him.

Paul in Philippians 1:29–30 says, "*For it has been granted to you that for the sake of Christ you should not only believe in him but also suffer for his sake, engaged in the same conflict that you saw I had and now hear that I still have*" (ESV).

His fellow Jews were rejecting the conflict that Paul experienced for becoming Christian. But their actions and comments did not deter Paul. He endured suffering so he could try to reach them with the gospel. We are engaged in the same conflict. The feeling of suffering diminishes when you take your focus off yourself and focus on sharing the good news of what Christ has done for you. Your friends have become distant because they do not know who Jesus is and what he has done in your life. When you suffer for the Lord, don't look at your own suffering for following Christ as discouraging. Be encouraged to tell your friends about Christ and what he has done in your life, knowing that suffering creates endurance.

3. Suffering Produces Many Positive Results

Suffering creates endurance that turns into trusting God more. Even though it's uncomfortable, suffering pushes and refocuses us on our dependency on God. Dependence on God will diminish grief, and we will rejoice in the positive outcomes suffering produces. Paul looked past his anguish and endured, knowing that the result would be worth the pain. Paul writes to Romans 5:3–5, "*We rejoice in our sufferings, knowing that suffering produces endurance, and endurance produces character, and character produces hope, and hope does not put us to shame, because God's love has been poured into our hearts through the Holy Spirit who has been given to us*" (ESV).

Because of this hope, we, too, can rejoice when we suffer for the gospel's sake and when we share our faith with others. Paul told the church in Colossae, "*I rejoice in my sufferings for your sake, and in my flesh, I am filling up what is lacking in Christ's afflictions for the sake of his body, that is, the church, of which I became a minister according to the stewardship from God that was given to me for you, to make the word of God fully known*" (Colossians 1:24–25 ESV).

As Christians, we will experience suffering. But when we do, we must understand that we suffer for God's kingdom mission. When

Walk to Finish Well

Paul wrote to Timothy, he had to remind him to be sober-minded and endure suffering to do the work of an evangelist. God commands Paul and Timothy to go out and preach the gospel (Acts 1:8). Have you ever suffered from sharing your faith with others? If you have not, you may not share your faith as much as you need to. Maybe you need to hear the exact words that Paul told Timothy. To do the work of an evangelist!

Do the Work of an Evangelist

Not all of us are chosen by God to be evangelists, but we are all called to evangelize. Paul wrote to the church in Ephesus and told them about the offices Christ had established within the church. *"Now these are the gifts Christ gave to the church: the apostles, the prophets, the evangelists, and the pastors and teachers"* (Ephesians 4:11 NLT).

The office of the evangelist is a spiritual gift that God has given to the church. An Evangelist is a gifted speaker who reaches an audience with the gospel. Billy Graham and Greg Laurie are current examples of evangelists who reach others with the gospel. In this context, Paul is not telling Timothy to become an evangelist but to do the "work" of an evangelist, mainly preaching the gospel.

We once heard the gospel of Christ and were saved by it. The gospel means "good news," and the good news is that Jesus died on the cross for our sins. Jesus was buried for three days and rose again, conquering sin and death. Because of Jesus's sacrifice, he saved those from sin and death who placed their faith in and believed in him. The gospel of Christ has affected us, and every Christian should do the work of an evangelist and proclaim the good news of our rescue.

Before Jesus ascended into heaven in Acts 1:8, he gave the apostles a command. Jesus said, *"But you will receive power when the Holy Spirit comes upon you. And you will be my witnesses, telling people about me everywhere—in Jerusalem, throughout Judea, in Samaria, and to the ends of the earth"* (NLT).

49

The apostles' mission was to tell people everywhere about Christ and the impact that the gospel made on their lives. That same mission was passed from generation to generation. When Paul wrote this letter to Timothy, he was close to death and wanted to convey to Timothy the importance of continuing to share the gospel. Timothy did not hold the office of an evangelist but had the same gospel message we have. We must share it and proclaim the good news of Jesus Christ.

How do we, as everyday Christians, proclaim the gospel? Think about eating at a great restaurant and having a wonderful meal. After the dinner, you would want to tell others how great the food tasted, the reasonable price, and how well you were treated. A friend at work went to a small steak house next to a strip mall that was not very well known, but the food was terrific. She went on and told me about it and that my wife and I should go. We can do the work of an evangelist by sharing our experiences and what being in a relationship with Jesus Christ has done for our lives. Give Jesus a five-star rating to your friends and recommend that they check him out.

Fulfill Your Ministry!

Our goal throughout life is to live a whole life, finish well, and fulfill the ministry God has given us. Have you ever considered what your ministry is? In our athlete's example, his ministry is to tell everyone within his sphere of influence what Jesus Christ has done in his life. His sphere of influence was who he trained with and the people he met during the competition. During the race, he will encounter many other athletes participating in their races, wanting to fulfill their goals. Along the way, our athlete will be a witness to others as he becomes an example of training his thoughts and his body to end well. The people around him will witness the suffering that he went through as he trained his body with weights in the gym, the countless hours on the lake swimming and the miles while running on foot and by bicycle.

Paul thought of his ministry just as Ironman did. Paul said,

> *"But my life is worth nothing to me unless I use it for finishing the work assigned me by the Lord Jesus—the work of telling others the Good News about the wonderful grace of God* (Acts 20:24 NLT).

The athlete will use his life to fulfill his ministry. When we opened this chapter, we talked about a youth at the beginning of the race, a middle-aged person running during the middle of the race, and an elderly person nearing the end of their race. If you are a youth, to fulfill your ministry is to reach your classmates, family members, and teachers with the good news of what Christ has done for you. If you are middle-aged, to fulfill your ministry is still to reach your family members, in-laws, coworkers, bosses, spouses, and children with the good news of what Christ has done for you. If you are elderly, fulfilling your ministry might require you to witness to your grandkids, children, in-laws, caretakers, spouses, and others within your sphere of influence with the gospel.

Running the race of life is not a sprint but a lifelong training and participating process. Throughout this process, our goal is to finish well. Why? So we can win that eternal prize waiting for us in heaven to be presented by Jesus himself. *"Don't you realize that in a race everyone runs, but only one person gets the prize? So run to win!"* says the apostle Paul. *"All athletes are disciplined in their training. They do it to win a prize that will fade away, but we do it for an eternal prize. So, I run with purpose in every step. I am not just shadowboxing"* (1 Corinthians 9:24–26 NLT).

Paul ran to win an eternal prize, and so should we. Paul had set his sights on the eternal reward, the crown of righteousness he would receive in heaven. Remember that when Paul was writing 2 Timothy, he was nearing the end of his race.

> *"And now the prize awaits me—the crown of righteousness, which the Lord, the righteous Judge, will give me on the day*

of his return. And the prize is not just for me but for all who eagerly look forward to his appearing" (2 Timothy 4:8 NLT).

When we get to heaven, we will receive the same reward and an even better reward when we hear the Lord speak these words. *"Well done, good and faithful servant. You have been faithful over a little; I will set you over much. Enter into the joy of your master"* (Matthew 25:23 ESV).

A Walk Exemplified

When I began this book, I mentioned that you could start here if you desired to strengthen your walk with Christ, but what if you do not know who Jesus is? What you have read in these pages can't be done alone. This book is not a self-help book on strengthening your walk with Christ apart from Christ. First, you must accept Jesus into your life as Savior and Lord. Then with the Holy Spirit's help, these truths can be applied to your walk. At the end of every podcast episode that Abiding in the Faith ministries has produced, I invite anyone listening to accept the Lord into their lives. I do this because you can't experience an abundant and full life apart from Jesus. So, I ask you, have you accepted the Lord Jesus as your Savior and Lord? If you have not, offer this simple prayer to the Lord:

> *Lord Jesus, I know I am a sinner in need of you. Thank you, Lord, for dying on the cross for my sins and rising from the dead to free me from my sins. I seek your forgiveness and choose to turn away from my sin to pursue you. Thank you for hearing and answering this prayer, in Jesus's name, Amen.*

If you have prayed this prayer with me, then welcome to the family of God!

We learned from Paul's life how to strengthen our walk with Jesus. But the best part is when we look at Jesus's life, we can see how he exemplified the principles we just learned about and how he can empower us to live this way.

Walk by Faith, Not Sight

In the first chapter, we looked at a model of walking by faith, not sight. We learned that faith is to have complete trust and confidence in Jesus Christ. Once we confirm the reliability of what we trust, we respond in faith. We can guarantee the reliability of Jesus from the biblical witnesses, evidence of his resurrection, and his existence.

As Christians, when we walk by faith and not sight, we walk to become molded into a life replicating Jesus Christ. Jesus exemplified walking by faith and not sight by fulfilling his primary purpose.

During Jesus's ministry here on earth, he referred to the purpose for which he came. While in the garden of Gethsemane, hours before his death on the cross, Jesus spoke to God in great anguish. Even in great need, Jesus prayed to God, knowing that death was at his doorstep. Jesus said, *"Now is my soul troubled. And what shall I say? 'Father, save me from this hour? But for this purpose, I have come to this hour* (John 12:27 ESV).

Jesus aimed to unite all things to God and could only do that by fulfilling God's purpose. A familiar passage in John explains Jesus's purpose. John writes, *"For God so loved the world, that he gave his only Son, that whoever believes in him should not perish but have eternal life. For God did not send his Son into the world to condemn the world, but so that the world might be saved through him"* (John 3:16–17 ESV)

Walk by the Spirit

We then examined what it means to walk by the Spirit, not the flesh. Jesus exemplified walking in the Spirit by following God's blueprint for his life. In John 6:38 NLT, John records Jesus's blueprint for his life that he followed. Jesus said, *"For I have come down from heaven to do the will of God who sent me, not to do my own will."*

In Luke 4:1, we read, *"Then Jesus, full of the Holy Spirit, returned from the Jordan River. He was led by the Spirit in the wilderness."* We can see from both verses that Jesus himself was led by the Spirit while walking in God's blueprint for his life. Jesus not only walked by the Spirit, but he had zeal.

Walk with Zeal

Jesus displayed zeal throughout his ministry, but there is one event to note. All three gospels record the event when Jesus cleansed the temple, but only the apostle John records the Lord's zeal. In John chapter 2:13–16, John records:

> It was nearly time for the Jewish Passover celebration, so Jesus went to Jerusalem. In the Temple area, he saw merchants selling cattle, sheep, and doves for sacrifices; he also saw dealers at tables exchanging foreign money. Jesus made a whip from some ropes and chased them all out of the temple. He drove out the sheep and cattle, scattered the money changers' coins over the floor, and turned over their tables. Then, going over to the people who sold doves, he told them, "Get these things out of here. Stop turning my Father's house into a marketplace!" (NLT).

Then his disciples remembered this prophecy from the Scriptures: "*Passion for God's house will consume me*" (John 2:17 NLT).

Walk in the Storm

Every storm has a beginning, a middle, and an end. We learned that it's better to go through a storm with Jesus than without him. The disciples were on a boat going across the Sea of Galilee to the opposite shoreline from where they were staying. As the boat headed out, Jesus went into the hull to nap. Suddenly, a storm came upon them, and the boat began to take in water during the storm. A few of the disciples were fishermen, becoming scared and worried their ship would sink. In desperation, they went down to Jesus and woke him up, "*shouting, 'Master, Master, we're going to drown!' When Jesus woke up, he rebuked the wind* and the raging waves. Suddenly the storm stopped and all was calm. Then he asked them, 'Where is your faith?' The disciples were terrified and amazed. 'Who is this man?' they asked each other. 'When he gives a command, even the wind and waves obey him!'" (Luke 8: 24–25 NLT).

Just as Jesus calmed the storm for the disciples, he can also calm the storm in your life. *"For in the day of trouble He will hide me in His shelter; He will conceal me under the cover of His tent; He will set me high upon a rock"* (Psalm 27:5 BSB). When Jesus is your Lord, he will hide and conceal you in his shelter. Jesus becomes *"…a booth for shade by day from the heat, and for a refuge and a shelter from the storm and rain"* (Isaiah 4:6 ESV).

Walk with Joy

We read that joy is found in partnership, prayer, living a life for Christ, and unity. Most importantly, our joy is found in Jesus Christ. Jesus exemplified joy by laying down his life for those who will find joy in him as the Lord of their life. Hebrews 12:1b–2 tells us that we should *"…run with endurance the race that is set before us, <u>looking to Jesus</u>, the founder, and perfecter of our faith, <u>who for the joy that was set before him endured the cross</u>, despising the shame, and is seated at the right hand of the throne of God"* (ESV, emphasis mine). The joy set before us is found in Jesus Christ, and we cannot find joy in anything we read or do without him. The Holy Spirit of God living inside us will produce joy and empower us to live this out.

Walk to Finish Well

Jesus relays the same sentiment as Paul in 1 Thessalonians 5:6 when he told the disciples to be ready for action. Jesus tells us to *"Be dressed for service and keep your lamps burning, as though you were waiting for your master to return from the wedding feast. Then you will be ready to open the door and let him in the moment he arrives and knocks. The servants who are ready and waiting for his return will be rewarded"* (Luke 12:35–37a NLT).

We can finish our race well when we stay sober-minded, ready for action, and powered by the Holy Spirit while we wait for Christ to return. By God's power, you can accomplish everything God has called you to do. No matter where you find yourself on this spiritual journey, young, old, or in between, it doesn't matter when you begin your race for Christ. It is how you finish the race of life that matters.

When we get to heaven, we will receive the same reward as Paul and an even better reward when we hear the Lord speak these words. *"Well done, good and faithful servant. You have been faithful over a little; I will set you over much. Enter into the joy of your master"* (Matthew 25:23 ESV).

Through Paul's writings, we get a small glimpse of how his walk with Jesus was strengthened as he imitated the life of Jesus. In 1 Corinthians 11:1, Paul wrote, *"Be imitators of me, as I am of Christ"* (ESV).

Paul worked hard to imitate Jesus daily with every thought and every action. Jesus's walk exemplified how we should go about our daily lives. We end in the words of Jesus from Matthew 28:19–20 NLT.

> *"Therefore, go and make disciples of all the nations, baptizing them in the name of the Father and the Son and the Holy Spirit. Teach these new disciples to obey all the commands I have given you. And be sure of this: I am with you always, even to the end of the age."*

Notes

1) Strong's Greek: 4102. πίστις (Pistis) – faith, faithfulness (biblehub.com).

2) Latto, 2022, "'I Feel Like My Purpose Is Bigger than Booty-Shaking Singles:' Latto Talks Leaving a Positive Impact on Women with Flaunt Magazine" (yahoo.com).

3) "What Is Sanctification? Bible Definition and Meaning" (biblestudytools.com).

4) "Zeal" Definition and meaning (Merriam-Webster).

5) Josephus, b. j. 4, 3, 9; 4, 5, 1; 4, 6, 3; 7, 8, 1.

Printed in the USA
CPSIA information can be obtained
at www.ICGtesting.com
CBHW020800020724
10943CB00001B/73